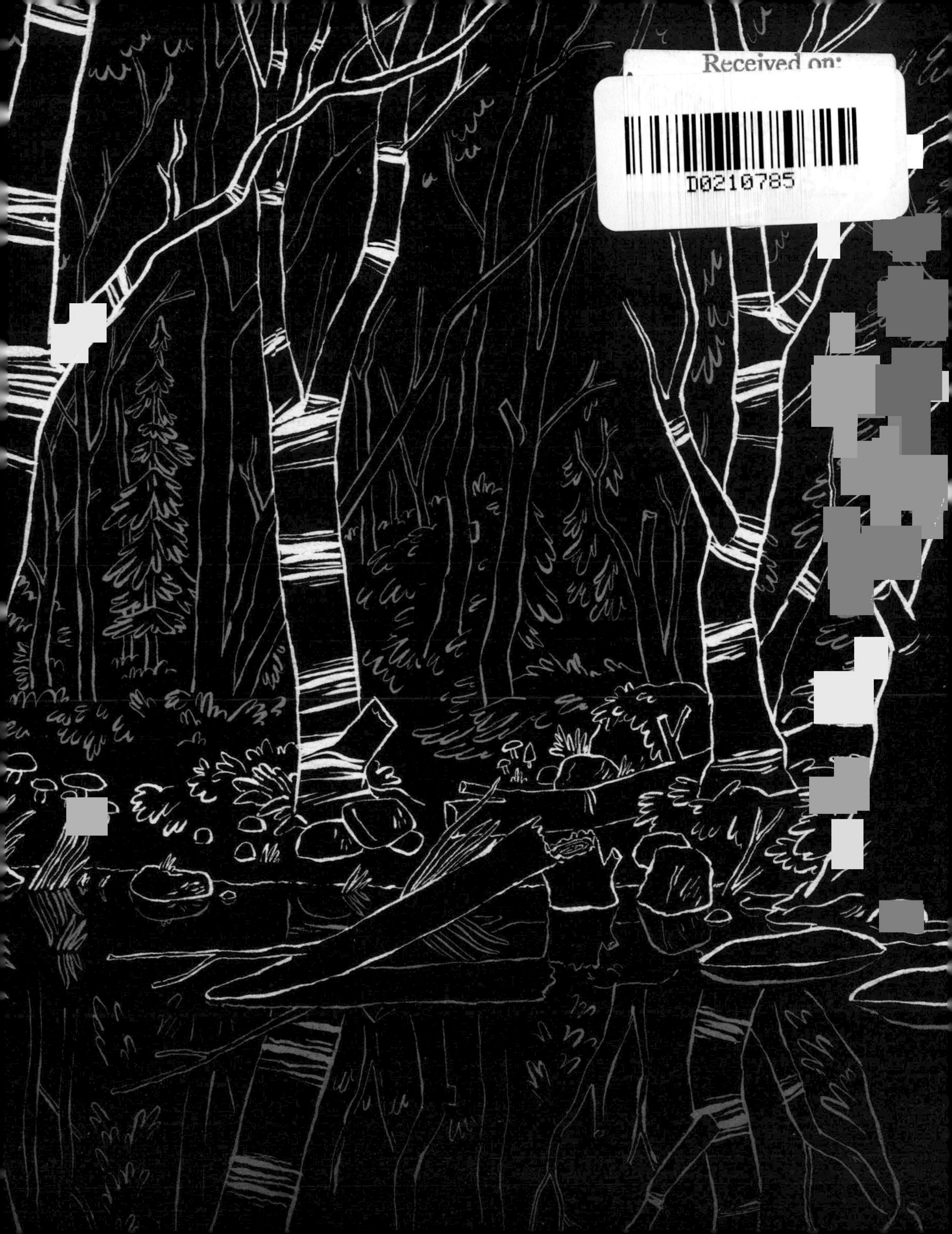

# DEEP DARK FEARS

FRAN KRAUSE

TEN SPEED PRESS
BERKELEY

# INTRODUCTION

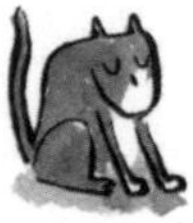

OH, HELLO! THANKS
FOR PICKING UP...

DEEP DARK FEARS!

I THOUGHT I'D TRY OUT
THIS FLASHLIGHT

...FOR DRAMATIC EFFECT!

I STARTED THIS COMIC BY TRYING TO DRAW ALL MY IRRATIONAL FEARS—

ACCIDENTALLY GETTING MY EYES POKED OUT, THAT SORT OF THING,

THEN PEOPLE STARTED SENDING IN THEIR OWN STORIES AND FEARS!

MY READERS HAVE BEEN VERY GENEROUS WITH THEIR STORIES,

AND I'VE REALLY LOVED DRAWING THEM!

SO, WELCOME! I HOPE YOU ENJOY...

DEEP DARK FEARS!

# FEAR #1

SOMETIMES WHEN I
SEE A MIRROR,

I PRESS MY FACE
AGAINST IT,

TRYING TO SEE AROUND THE CORNER.

I'M SURE THERE'S SOMETHING HIDING JUST OUT OF SIGHT.

# FEAR #2

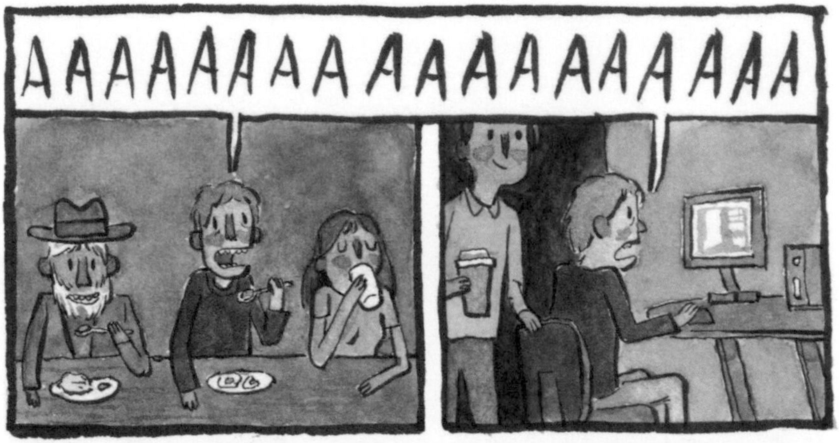
AAAAAAAAAAAAAAAA

SOMETIMES I WORRY I'M ACTUALLY SCREAMING CONSTANTLY,

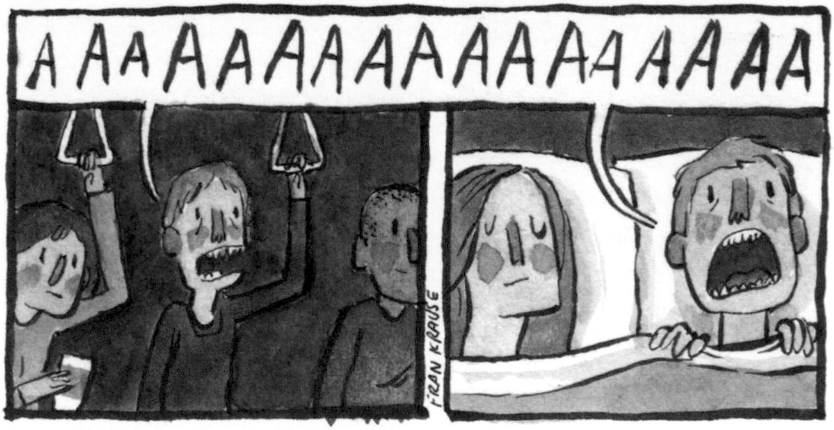
AAAAAAAAAAAAAAAAA
FRAN KRAUSE

AND PEOPLE JUST PRETEND I'M NORMAL.

# FEAR #3

BE CAREFUL WITH YOUR ARMS AND LEGS.

NEVER LET THEM HANG OFF THE BED.

ABOVE YOU, THERE IS AN INVISIBLE GUILLOTINE,

WAITING FOR YOU TO ISSUE A CHALLENGE.

# FEAR #4

IT'S SUMMERTIME, AND I'M DRIVING WITH MY WINDOWS OPEN!

THE WIND BLOWS AROUND SOME JUNK IN MY BACKSEAT.

A PLASTIC BAG GETS
BLOWN OVER MY HEAD
AND I SUFFOCATE.

THE POLICE WHO
RESPOND KINDA
HAVE A CHUCKLE.

# FEAR #5

WHEN I GO BOWLING,

I WORRY THAT MY FINGERS WILL GET STUCK IN THE BALL,

AND THE WEIGHT OF THE BALL WILL RIP THEM OFF,

AND I WON'T EVEN KNOCK OVER ANY PINS.

# FEAR #6

ON THE INSIDE, YOU'RE A ROBOT.

YOU'VE ALWAYS BEEN A ROBOT.

BACK WHEN YOU WERE MADE, ROBOTS WERE CLUNKY AND CRUDE,

SO, OUT OF PITY, EVERYONE PRETENDS THAT YOU PASS FOR HUMAN.

# FEAR #7

I WORRY THAT THE ICE
WILL OPEN UP,

I'LL FALL INTO THE
FREEZING WATER,

AND THE CURRENT WILL CARRY ME
AWAY FROM THE HOLE.

# FEAR #8

DAD TOLD ME THAT KIDS WERE BORN WHEN A DAD GAVE A MOM A SPECIAL HUG.

A BIG HUG!

FOR MONTHS AFTERWARDS,

I REFUSED TO HUG ANY MEN.

# FEAR #9

SOMETIMES I RUN AND I RUN,

AND I *JUST* MAKE THE TRAIN,

AND I IMMEDIATELY WORRY THAT I WAS *MEANT* TO MISS IT,

AND IT'S GOING TO CRASH AT THE NEXT STOP.

# FEAR #10

ONCE, WHEN I WAS A YOUNG KID IN NEW ENGLAND, I WAS PICKING BLACKBERRIES IN THE WOODS.

I ATE ONE, SEEDS AND ALL.

AN OLDER KID TOLD ME THAT THE SEED WOULD NEVER DIGEST.

IT WOULD GROW AS A THORNY VINE ALONG MY ARTERIES.

THE VINES WOULD TURN TO WOOD, AND IT WOULD BECOME PAINFUL TO MOVE.

HE ADDED THAT IT WOULD BE VERY EXPENSIVE TO TREAT,

PAT PAT PAT

SO BETTER NOT TO BOTHER MY PARENTS ABOUT ANYTHING AND JUST DEAL WITH IT.

I DIDNT SLEEP FOR WEEKS.

# FEAR #11

MY DAD TOLD ME TO STAY
AWAY FROM SWEETS
BEFORE BED.

HE TOLD ME ABOUT A GIRL
WHO HAD GONE TO SLEEP
WITH A LOLLYPOP IN HER MOUTH.

OVER THE FOLLOWING WEEK
SHE HAD HEADACHES.

ANTS HAD TURNED HER
HEAD INTO AN ANT FARM.

# FEAR #12

WHEN I'M HUGGING MY BOYFRIEND,

I FEEL SO CRAZED WITH AFFECTION,

LIKE I NEED TO DIG INTO HIS BODY,

AND LIVE INSIDE HIM.

# FEAR #13

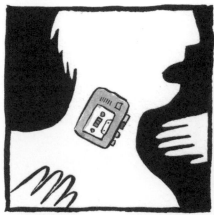

I USED TO THINK MY VOICE BOX WAS LIKE A CASSETTE TAPE,

AND IT RECORDED EVERYTHING I SAID,

AND IF I SAID SOMETHING BAD,

IT COULD BE REMOVED TO REPEAT MY OLD WORDS.

# FEAR # 14

SOMETIMES I THINK THAT I'LL GROW TOO BIG,

INTO THE SKY, LIKE A GIANT.

THE AIR WILL GROW THIN
AROUND MY HEAD,

AND I'LL SUFFOCATE
IN THE STARS.

FRAN KRAUSE

# FEAR # 15

LATE AT NIGHT, WHEN I'M ALONE,

I HEAR QUIET VOICES CALLING MY NAME.

I WORRY THAT MY LIFE IS A DREAM, I'm REALLY IN A COMA,

AND THE VOICES ARE MY FAMILY TRYING TO WAKE ME UP.

# FEAR # 16

WHEN I WAS A KID, A PRIEST TOLD ME ABOUT MARY,

HOW GOD THOUGHT SHE WAS PERFECT, SO HE MADE HER PREGNANT.

I DIDN'T WANT GOD TO MAKE ME PREGNANT,

SO I TRIED TO NOT BE HIS TYPE.

# FEAR # 17

I WORRY THAT MY
REFLECTION IS RECORDING
MY EXPRESSIONS,

AND ONE DAY WHEN
IT HAS CAPTURED
THEM ALL,

IT WILL CRAWL OUT
OF THE MIRROR,

AND IT WILL
REPLACE ME.

# FEAR #18

I WORRY THAT I'LL FALL

AND BITE OFF MY TONGUE,

AND WHEN I CALL 911,

THEY WON'T BE ABLE
TO UNDERSTAND ME.

# FEAR #19

I'M AFRAID THAT ONE DAY, I'LL TOUCH MY FACE,

AND IT WILL BE SOFT, LIKE CLAY.

I'LL TRY TO PUT IT BACK TO NORMAL,

BUT I'LL WIND UP LOOKING LIKE A PICASSO.

# FEAR #20

WHEN I WAS LITTLE
I WAS AFRAID

THAT MY DOLLS
WOULD WATCH ME SLEEP,

SO I WOULD COVER
THEIR CRADLE WITH
A BLANKET

AND A PILE OF BOOKS
SO THEY COULDN'T
ESCAPE.

# FEAR #21

I WORRY THAT I'LL BE RESTING MY FEET
ON THE DASHBOARD AND BE IN AN ACCIDENT,

AND THE CRASH WON'T BE TOO BAD, BUT
I'LL DIE WHEN THE AIR BAG MAKES ME
KNEE MYSELF IN THE FACE.

# FEAR #22

SOMETIMES I FEEL
LIKE PEOPLE ARE
READING MY MIND,

SO I THINK OF
SOMETHING FUNNY.

THAT WAY, IF I
HEAR ANYONE LAUGH,

I KNOW.

# FEAR #23

I'M AFRAID THAT ONE NIGHT,

I'LL TRY TO TAKE OUT
MY CONTACT LENS,

BUT I'LL FORGET THAT I'M
NOT WEARING THEM,

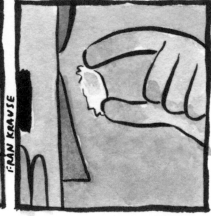

AND I'LL ACCIDENTALY
PULL OFF MY CORNEA.

# FEAR #24

EVERY TIME I TELL SOMEONE "I LOVE YOU,"

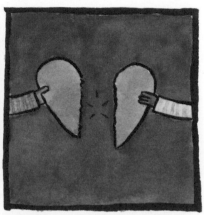

MY SOUL IS SPLIT IN HALF.

I WORRY THAT SOMEDAY,

I'LL HAVE NONE LEFT.

# FEAR #25

IF YOU'RE MAKING OUT ON THE BUS,

BUT THE DRIVER'S NOT CAREFUL,

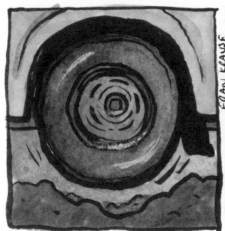

THEY MIGHT HIT A BIG BUMP,

AND YOU'D BITE EACH OTHER'S TONGUES OFF.

# FEAR #26

SOMETIMES I WORRY

I'M DELUSIONAL,

AND MY DOG

IS ACTUALLY A PILE
OF LAUNDRY IN THE
PSYCH WARD.

# FEAR # 27

WHEN I CLEAN MY EAR
WITH A Q-TIP, I WORRY
THAT SOMEONE WILL OPEN
THE BATHROOM DOOR

AND BUMP THE Q-TIP
INTO MY BRAIN.

SO, WHEN I CLEAN MY EARS, I LOCK THE DOOR,

AND I STAND IN THE BATHTUB WITH ALL MY CLOTHES ON.

# FEAR # 28

WHEN I BAKE COOKIES, I'm CAREFUL TO CLEAN UP.

OTHERWISE I MIGHT STEP ON A COOKIE CUTTER

AND GET A WIERD HOLE IN MY FOOT.

# FEAR #29

JESUS LIVES INSIDE YOU!
HE LIVES DEEP INSIDE YOUR HEART.
INRI
FRAN KRAUSE

# FEAR #30

I WORRY THAT SOMEONE'S GOING TO RUSH BEHIND ME WITH AN EMPTY HAND TRUCK

AND THE SHARP EDGE WILL SLICE MY ACHILLES TENDONS.

# FEAR #31

WHEN MY DOGS WANT
TO COME INSIDE,

I NEED TO CHECK
THE WHOLE HOUSE,

LOOKING FOR MY DOGS,

IN CASE THE ONES OUTSIDE
ARE SHAPESHIFTERS.

# FEAR #32

WHEN I WAS A KID, MY GRANDMOTHER TOLD ME THAT EVERYONE HAS A CERTAIN NUMBER OF BREATHS.

NOBODY KNOWS THEIR NUMBER, BUT WHEN YOU RUN OUT OF BREATHS, YOU DIE.

SO I SPENT MY TIME TRYING TO BREATHE SLOWLY,

HOPING TO MAKE EACH ONE LAST.

# FEAR #33

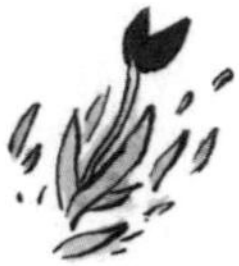

I WORRY A STRONG WAVE WILL HIT AND
TURN ME AROUND. I'LL TRY TO GET BACK
TO SHORE, NOT KNOWING THAT I'M ONLY
SWIMMING FARTHER OUT TO SEA.

# FEAR #34

I DON'T LIKE WHEN MY TEACHER RETURNS HOMEWORK.

I'M NOT WORRIED ABOUT MY GRADE,

IT'S JUST THAT HE HOLDS OUR PAPERS AT EYE LEVEL,

AND ALL I CAN THINK ABOUT IS PAPER CUTS.

# FEAR #35

I USED TO THINK THAT
WHEN I CLOSED A BOOK,

ALL THE CHARACTERS
WOULD FREEZE IN PLACE,

AND IF I LEFT THEM
FOR TOO LONG,

THEY COULD GET UP
TO MISCHIEF.

FRAN KRAUSE

# FEAR # 36

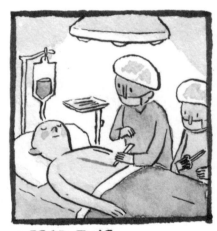

I FEAR THAT,

IN THE MIDDLE OF SURGERY,

THE POWER WILL GO OUT    FOR A LONG TIME.

# FEAR # 37

WHEN I WAS A KID, I
KNEW WHERE BABIES
CAME FROM,

THEY CAME OUT OF
YOUR BUTT!

EVEN THOUGH I'M A BOY,
I ALWAYS CHECKED MY POOPS,

TO MAKE SURE I DIDN'T
HAVE ANY BABIES.

# FEAR #38

I WORRY THAT, AFTER I DIE,

ALL MY SENSES WILL CONTINUE TO WORK.

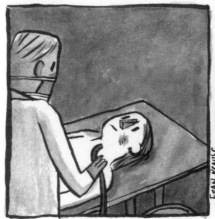

I DON'T KNOW IF ENBALMING

WOULD BE WORSE THAN CREMATION.

# FEAR # 39

MY MOM SAID SHE HAD
TO BE CAREFUL OF BRIGHT
LIGHTS WHILE DRIVING.

AT NIGHT, SOMEONE'S
HIGH BEAMS MIGHT
BLIND YOU.

I THOUGHT SHE MEANT
PERMANENTLY, SO I SHUT
MY EYES AND PREPARED,

IN CASE MY MOM
WAS BLINDED AND I
HAD TO TAKE THE WHEEL.

# FEAR # 40

IN THE COLD WINTER AIR, MY BREATH BECOMES VISIBLE.

I HOPE IT DOESN'T MEAN THAT PEOPLE SEE MY FARTS.

# FEAR # 41

WHEN I CAN'T KEEP FROM YAWNING,

I KNOW THERE ARE GHOSTS IN MY ROOM,

OPENING MY MOUTH,

TO SEE IF THEIR HANDS FIT INSIDE.

# FEAR #42

WHEN I WAS LITTLE, I WASN'T ALLOWED TO
WATCH "DRACULA," BECAUSE IT WAS TOO SCARY.

AT NIGHT I'D STILL HAVE NIGHTMARES, WHERE DRACULA WAS A BIG ROBOT, BECAUSE I HAD NO IDEA WHAT A "DRACULA" WAS.

# FEAR #43

WHEN I SAY "HELLO" TO PEOPLE, AND THEY DON'T RESPOND,

I WORRY THAT I'M DEAD, AND I JUST DON'T KNOW YET.

# FEAR #44

IT GETS REALLY ICY
IN BROOKLYN.

I WORRY I'LL SLIP

AND GOUGE MY EYES ON
A WROUGHT IRON FENCE,

AND IT'LL BE TOO SLIPPERY
TO FREE MYSELF.

# FEAR #45

THERE IS AN OLD ARCHWAY AT THE ENTRANCE TO MY SCHOOL.

IF YOU STAND BENEATH IT AT NIGHT WITH YOUR EYES CLOSED,

YOU'LL FEEL SOMETHING
TAP YOUR HEAD.

IT'S THE FEET OF A
STUDENT WHO HANGED
HIMSELF FROM THE
ARCH LONG AGO.

# FEAR #46

I LIVE ALONE.

WHEN I HAVE TO GO
TO THE BATHROOM
LATE AT NIGHT,

I WORRY THAT WHEN
I GO BACK TO BED,

SOMEONE WILL BE
WAITING THERE.

# FEAR # 47

DEATH IS A THEATER,

FULL OF EVERYONE YOU'VE EVER MET,

WATCHING A REAL-TIME REPLAY OF YOUR LIFE,

WITH YOUR EVERY THOUGHT NARRATED OUT LOUD.

# FEAR # 48

I DON'T LIKE BEING TOO CLOSE TO SHARP KNIVES.

SO I PUSH THEM AWAY,

TILL THEY'RE JUST OUT OF REACH.

FRAN KRAUSE

# FEAR #49

I SAW MY PARENTS FLUSH A PET FISH DOWN THE TOILET.

AFTER THAT,

I THOUGHT THAT WHEN PEOPLE DIED,

THEY WOULD BE FLUSHED DOWN THE TOILET TOO.

# FEAR # 50

I NEED TO GET TO THE
BATHROOM, BUT MY ROOM
IS FULL OF GHOSTS.

I MAKE A DISGUISE
WITH MY SHEETS,

SO I CAN MOVE
AMONG THEM,

TOTALLY UNDETECTED.

# FEAR #51

GHOSTS LIVED AT THE END
OF MY STREET.

I CHALLENGED THEM TO
A RACE.

IF THEY BEAT ME HOME, THEY COULD STAY THERE FOREVER.

CONTINUED...

I TURNED TO SEE HOW FAR THE GHOSTS WERE LAGGING BEHIND,

JUST AS A STRONG GUST PUSHED PAST ME, THROUGH THE DOOR,

FRAN KRAUSE

# FEAR #52

WHEN I WAKE UP,

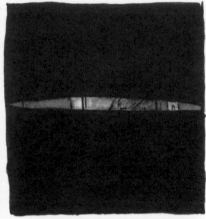

I OPEN MY EYES VERY SLOWLY,

SO ANYTHING THAT MAY BE IN MY ROOM

HAS A CHANCE TO HIDE.

# FEAR #53

MY MOM TOLD ME THAT, IF I RODE THE ESCALATOR WITH MY SHOES UNTIED,

IT WOULD GRAB THE LACES AND SUCK ME UNDER.

SHE SAID ALL THE MALL COPS WERE KIDS WHO GOT SUCKED INTO THE ESCALATOR AND HAD TO STAY FOREVER.

# FEAR # 54

MY PARENTS TOLD ME

THAT FOG WAS A CLOUD

THAT CAME DOWN FROM
THE SKY

AND TOOK AWAY BAD
CHILDREN.

# FEAR #55

AT NIGHT,

MY BED BECOMES A
RAFT, LOST AT SEA.

MY WALLS

BECOME TOWERING WAVES
SURROUNDING MY CRAFT.

# FEAR #56

EACH ONE OF US HAS OUR OWN INDIVIDUAL
DEATH GOD, WHO FOLLOWS US WHEREVER WE
GO, WAITING TO KILL US AT A PREDETERMINED
MOMENT. WHEN THE TIME COMES, WE'LL
FINALLY BE ABLE TO SEE THEM AS THEY TAKE
US TO THE OTHER SIDE.

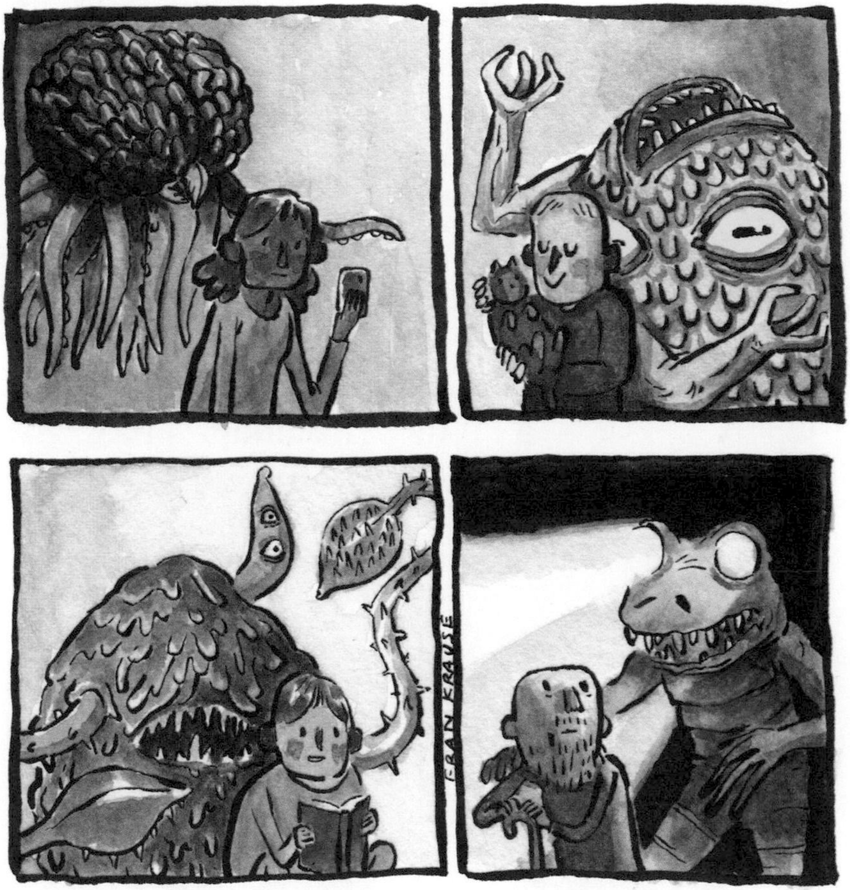
ERAN KRAUSE

# FEAR #57

WHEN I PLUCK A HAIR, I WORRY THAT
IT'LL KEEP GOING AND GOING UNTIL
SOMETHING UNRAVELS INSIDE ME.

# FEAR #58

ONE DAY I'LL BE FACEBOOK-STALKING SOMEONE,

AND I'LL ACCIDENTALLY TYPE THEIR NAME INTO "UPDATE STATUS" INSTEAD OF THE SEARCH BOX,

AND THEY'LL BE AUTOMATICALLY TAGGED IN THE POST,

AND I WON'T NOTICE UNTIL EVERYONE ELSE SEES IT.

# FEAR # 59

THERE IS A MIRROR IN MY BEDROOM.
I WORRY THAT, WHILE I SLEEP,

MY REFLECTION SITS UP AND WATCHES ME.

# FEAR # 60

I HELPED A FRIEND PUT
IN THEIR AIR CONDITIONER.

IT WEIGHED A LOT.

ALMOST AS MUCH AS ME.

I'M GLAD I DIDN'T
DROP IT ON MY FOOT
OR ANYTHING.

# FEAR #61

I HAVE BAD DREAMS,

WHERE MY TEETH GO LOOSE,

BUT I HAVE BRACES,

AND THEY ALL COME OUT LIKE A STRING OF PEARLS.

# FEAR # 62

MY FRIEND TOLD ME THAT
BIRTHMARKS SHOW HOW YOU
DIED IN YOUR LAST LIFE.

A LITTLE FRECKLE ON
YOUR ARM MIGHT MEAN
IT WAS AN INJECTION.

A DIME-SIZED MARK
MIGHT BE FROM A BULLET.

MINE IS BIG. I DON'T
WANT TO KNOW WHAT
HAPPENED TO ME.

# FEAR #63

I FEAR THAT, ONE DAY,

I'LL HEAR MY MOTHER'S VOICE CALLING FOR HELP FROM THE ATTIC,

BUT ON THE WAY THERE, SHE'LL PULL ME ASIDE,

BECAUSE SHE HEARD IT TOO.

# FEAR #64

WHEN I'M LOOKING INTO A MIRROR, I WORRY THAT SOMETHING'S BEHIND ME,

BUT IT'S THE SAME SIZE AS ME, AND IT MOVES ALONG WITH ME,

SO I NEVER SEE IT,

BUT IT'S ALWAYS THERE.

# FEAR #65

WHEN YOU ARE DEAD AND BURIED,

YOUR SPIRIT WILL CLIMB THE NEAREST TREE, TRYING TO REACH HEAVEN.

THE CLIMB TAKES YEARS.

EVERY TREE IN THE CEMETERY HAS A GHOST INSIDE.

# FEAR #66

I KEEP MY SCISSORS INSIDE A LOCKED BOX,

SO I WON'T DO ANYTHING WITH THEM WHEN I SLEEPWALK.

# FEAR #67

ONE DAY, YOU'LL HAVE AN ACCIDENT.

YOU'LL BE UNCONSIOUS FOR A WHILE, OR IN A COMA.

YOUR CAT WILL GET HUNGRY,

AND IT WILL EAT YOUR LIPS AND EYELIDS.

# FEAR #68

MY FAMILY WENT ON A
ROAD TRIP,

FAR OUT INTO THE
COUNTRY.

WE FOUND A BIG OLD HOTEL, SURROUNDED BY FORESTS.

MY SISTER AND I EXPLORED THE HALLWAYS.

WE FOUND A BANQUET ROOM THAT WAS EMPTY,

EXCEPT FOR A SINGLE OLD MAN. HE TURNED AND SMILED AT US BUT SAID NOTHING.

CONTINUED...

LATER THAT NIGHT, I GOT
UP TO CLOSE MY WINDOW,

AND I SAW THE OLD MAN
WALKING ALONE IN THE FOG.

HE TOOK A THIN PATH INTO
THE WOODS AND VANISHED.

I STAYED UP FOR HOURS
BUT HE NEVER CAME BACK.

EARLY THE NEXT MORNING, I SNUCK OUT OF MY ROOM,

AND I FOLLOWED THE PATH INTO THE WOODS.

IT TOOK ME TO A SMALL, OVERGROWN GRAVEYARD AND ENDED THERE.

# FEAR # 69

I'VE ALWAYS BEEN
AFRAID THAT SOMEWHERE,

FUTURE TIME TRAVELERS
FLIP THROUGH OUR MIRRORS

AS IF THEY WERE
T.V. SCREENS,

CATCHING OUR MOST
AWKWARD AND PERSONAL
MOMENTS.

# FEAR # 70

SOMETIMES WHEN I'M POOPING, I WORRY THAT, AT THAT MOMENT,

IT'S A DREAM, AND I'M REALLY POOPING MY PANTS SOMEWHERE.

# FEAR # 71

I'M AFRAID OF THE THING UNDER MY BED,

BUT THERE IS ONLY A THIN SPACE,

SO I AM AFRAID OF THE FLAT MAN BENEATH MY BED.

# FEAR # 72

I HOPE I DON'T EVER TURN INTO AN OLD PERSON
WHO MAKES KIDS AFRAID OF GETTING OLD.

# FEAR #73

WHEN I WAS LITTLE,

MY MOM TOLD ME THAT
IF I KEPT WETTING MY BED,

WORMS WOULD GROW OUT OF
MY MATTRESS,

AND THEY'D EAT ME ALIVE.

# FEAR # 74

WHEN I WAS YOUNGER, I WORRIED THAT WHEN I DIED,

I'D BECOME AN EXTRA IN OTHER PEOPLE'S DREAMS.

SOMETIMES I FEEL
THAT ALL THE PEOPLE
IN MY DREAMS

ARE DEAD AND
HAVE NOWHERE
ELSE TO GO.

# FEAR #75

WHEN I WAS A LITTLE KID,

MY AUNT TOLD ME THAT IF I STEPPED ON A NEEDLE,

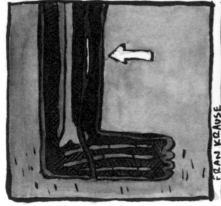

IT WOULD FOLLOW MY VEINS

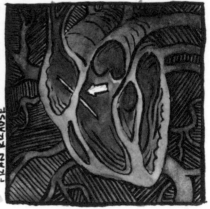

STRAIGHT TO MY HEART.

# FEAR #76

I CAN'T EAT, TOUCH, OR LOOK AT MUSHROOMS.

I'M TOO SCARED THAT THE SPORES...

...WILL SEED INTO MY SKIN AND GROW.

# FEAR # 77

WHEN I WAS A KID, I
SAW PHOTOS OF THE
TITANIC UNDERWATER.

I THOUGHT OF WHAT IT
WOULD BE LIKE TO CLOSE
MY EYES AND FIND
MYSELF ON THE DECK,

KNOWING THAT I WAS
UNDER TWO MILES
OF BLACK WATER.

# FEAR # 78

THERE WERE MASKS ON
THE WALLS OF MY AUNT'S
GUEST BEDROOM.

AT NIGHT, I'D IMAGINE
THAT THEY'D PULL
ME INTO THE WALL,

UP TO MY NECK,

AND THEN THEY'D
COVER ME WITH
A NEW MASK.

FRAN KRAUSE

# FEAR # 79

I'M NOT WAVING AT ANYONE,

AND I'M NOT CRAZY.

I'M JUST MAKING SURE THERE ARE NO

INVISIBLE PEOPLE IN MY BATHROOM.

# FEAR #80

IN THE FUTURE, I'LL
GET A TELEPORTER,

AND I'LL TELEPORT
SOMEWHERE FUN,

BUT SOMEONE WILL
ALREADY BE THERE,

AND WE'LL BE STUCK
TOGETHER FOREVER.

# FEAR # 81

WHEN I WAS A KID I WORRIED
THAT WHEN I WOKE UP,

I'D FIND MY FAMILY HAVING
BREAKFAST WITH MY DOPPELGÄNGER,

WE WOULD FIGHT TO
THE DEATH,

AND THEN MY FAMILY WOULD
PEACEFULLY FINISH BREAKFAST.

# FEAR #82

I WORRY THAT,

AT MY FUNERAL,

NOBODY WILL HAVE
GOOD STORIES

OR NICE THINGS
TO SAY.

# FEAR # 83

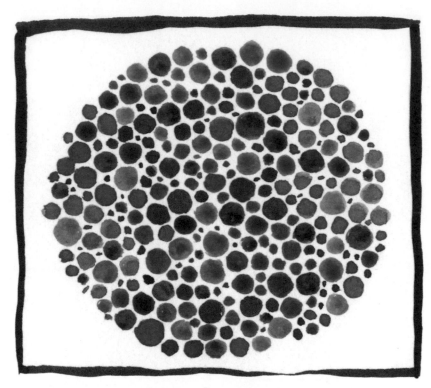

IF YOU SEE A NUMBER IN
THIS CIRCLE, YOU CAN
SEE GHOSTS.

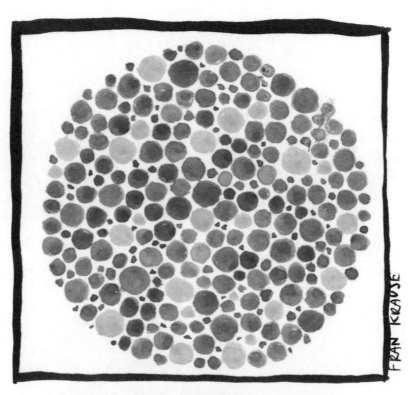

IF YOU SEE A NUMBER IN THIS
CIRCLE, YOU CAN TELL GOOD
GHOSTS APART FROM EVIL GHOSTS.

# FEAR #84

WHEN I WAS LITTLE AND PLAYED ALL DAY IN THE SUN,

I'D SEE LITTLE WHITE DOTS FLOATING BEFORE MY EYES.

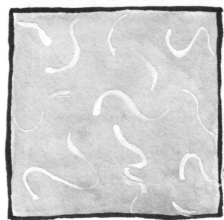

I THOUGHT THEY WERE TINY PARASITES,

SLOWLY EATING MY EYEBALLS.

# FEAR #85

I HAVE A DEAL WORKED
OUT WITH THE THINGS THAT
HIDE IN MY BASEMENT.

AFTER I SHUT OFF THE
LIGHTS, I HAVE EXACTLY TEN
SECONDS TO LEAVE SAFELY.

I ALWAYS USE THE FULL
TEN SECONDS,

HOPING TO SEE A FLASH
OF MOVEMENT JUST AS I
REACH SAFETY.

# FEAR #86

WHEN I REACH OUT TO OPEN A "PULL" DOOR,

I WORRY THAT SOMEONE IS ON THE OTHER SIDE, ABOUT TO KICK IT OPEN.

# FEAR #87

EVER SINCE MY
FRIEND TOLD ME

SHE COULD WIGGLE
HER KNEECAPS,

I WORRY THAT I'LL
WIGGLE MINE,

AND THEY'LL SLIP
DOWN MY LEGS.

# FEAR #88

WHEN I WAS 9, MY COUSIN TOLD ME THAT IF I SLEPT ON MY LEFT SIDE,

MY OTHER ORGANS WOULD CRUSH MY HEART.

I ALWAYS SLEEP ON MY RIGHT SIDE.

# FEAR #89

IF I DIE IN MY SLEEP, I HOPE I DRIFT OFF TO A FLYING DREAM,

AND NOT THAT ONE I ALWAYS HAVE ABOUT FLOORPLANS.

# FEAR # 90

BAREFOOT, CARRYING DIRTY
DISHES TO THE KITCHEN
IN THE DARK,

I WORRY THAT I'LL
DROP THEM.

THEN I'LL BE STUCK,
SURROUNDED BY INVISIBLE
SHARDS OF GLASS,

WAITING FOR SUNRISE.

FRAN KRAUSE

# FEAR # 91

I WORRY THAT MY PETS ARE REINCARNATED
RELATIVES, HORRIFIED BY MY PRIVATE MOMENTS.

AND IF THEY ENJOY WATCHING? EVEN WORSE.

# FEAR # 92

WHEN I'M GOING TO THE
KITCHEN LATE AT NIGHT,

I TRY TO ACT FUNNY
AND CHARMING.

THAT WAY, ANY MURDERERS
LOOKING IN MY WINDOWS

WILL THINK I'M TOO
NICE TO KILL.

# FEAR #93

I HAVE A NIGHTMARE. I'M IN AN EXPANDING ROOM.

I WALK FOR HOURS, BUT NEVER REACH THE DOOR.

# FEAR #94

IT'S MY JOB TO TAKE THE GARBAGE TO THE TRASH COMPACTOR.

I ALWAYS FEEL LIKE SOMEONE WILL SNEAK UP AND PUSH ME IN.

WHEN THE DOOR CLOSES, IT AUTOMATICALLY LOCKS AND STARTS COMPACTING.

THE ONLY WAY TO SHUT IT OFF IS WITH THE KEY IN MY POCKET.

# FEAR #95

I WORRY THAT, WHEN I DIE, IT WON'T HAPPEN ALL AT ONCE.

IT'LL START AT MY FEET,

FRAN KRAUSE

AND I'LL FEEL IT WORKING ITS WAY UP.

# FEAR # 96

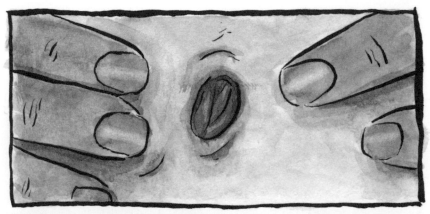

WHEN I WAS LITTLE, MY GRANDMA TOLD ME IF I PLAYED WITH MY BELLY BUTTON,

ALL MY GUTS WOULD FALL OUT, AND I'D HAVE TO CARRY THEM AROUND FOR THE REST OF MY LIFE IN A LAUNDRY BASKET.

# FEAR # 97

WHAT IF MY WISHES FOR IMMORTALITY WERE GRANTED,

BUT ONLY FOR ME?

I'D SEE THE FUTURE,

AND I'D LIVE TO SEE IT CRUMBLE.

I'D LIVE TO SEE THE
EARTH BURN,

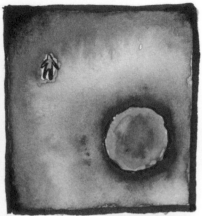

AND THE SUN GROW
OLD.

I'D WATCH EACH STAR
WINK OUT OF EXISTENCE,

KNOWING I HAD ONLY
LIVED A SPECK OF
ETERNITY.

# FEAR #98

AFTER THE FUNERAL,

I'D WORRY IT WAS ALL FAKE.

MY LOVED ONE HADN'T ACTUALLY DIED.

THEY JUST WANTED TO ESCAPE AND START OVER.

# FEAR # 99

WHENEVER I TAKE THE
ELEVATOR,

I WORRY AS I STEP
OFF

THAT THE ELEVATOR
WILL DROP

AND CUT ME IN HALF.

# FEAR #100

MY DAD SAID FLASHLIGHT BEAMS NEVER ENDED.

SOMEDAY MINE WOULD BE SEEN BY ALIENS.

I SENT THEM A MESSAGE.

# FEAR #101

I WORRY THAT MY LIFE IS AN ILLUSION.

IT'S ALL A DREAM.

I WORRY I'LL WAKE UP SOMEDAY AND REALIZE

I'M JUST A VERY IMAGINATIVE DOG.

# ABOUT THE AUTHOR

FRAN KRAUSE WAS BORN IN UPSTATE NEW YORK,
BUT NOW LIVES IN LOS ANGELES WITH
HIS WIFE JOANNA AND A CAT NAMED CAT CAT.
HE TEACHES ANIMATION AT CALARTS AND LIKES
DRAWING COMICS AND RIDING HIS BIKE.

# ACKNOWLEDGMENTS

FOR JOANNA, MY #1 FAN.

THANK YOU KAITLIN KETCHUM AND
BETSY STROMBERG AT TEN SPEED PRESS.

# I'D LIKE TO EXTEND MY THANKS TO EVERYONE WHO SHARED THEIR FEARS WITH ME.

FEAR #1 - JOANNA, #2 - ANONYMOUS, #3 - AUDREY, #5 - NAOMI, #6 - ANONYMOUS, #7 - ANONYMOUS, #8 - ANONYMOUS, #9 - ANONYMOUS, #10 - ANONYMOUS, #11 - 8BITUNICORN, #12 - KATE, #13 - VEGANNERVEPINCH, #14 - THE FLO FIC, #15 - BLANE2256, #16 - ANONYMOUS, #17 - LIAMKRUGER, #18 - MICHAEL, #19 - G3NIES, #20 - CRAZYCOSTUMEDKITTY, #21 - ELEANORNOTRIGBY, #22 - ANONYMOUS, #23 - YEJILEE, #24 - ATAMAJAKKI, #25 - ANONYMOUS, #26 - HOLLY, #27 - CYRANOTORUS, #28 - RILEY, #29 - DONOVIC AND JUMBLE-IT-UP, #30 - PES, #31 - ANONYMOUS, #32 - MARCUS, #33 - BLUE-SKYFIRE, #34 - HEIDI, #35 - DAREANDWRITEITDOWN, #36 - ANONYMOUS, #37 - THE-ADVENTUROUS-GOUL, #38 - MIAUMIOU, #39 - SCHOLARLYPHASES, #40 - EZEQUIEL, #41 - EVELYN-ISNOTREAL, #42 - MELANIE, #43 - COZIESTBEAN, #44 - LIZZI, #45 - ANONYMOUS, #46 - CITIZENPIONEER, #47 - LIZ PRINCE, #48 - ANONYMOUS, #49 - PLATYPOOSE, #50 - APRIL, #51 - MAKIISHIMAA, #52 - ACHROMUS, #53 - MOUNT, #54 - ANONYMOUS, #55 - BIGFACEALLOVERTHEPLACE, #56 - ANONYMOUS, #57 - RAFE-ALECARDI, #58 - ANONYMOUS, #59 - ANONYMOUS, #60 - SYDNEY, #61 - TOODLELIU, #62 - ANONYMOUS, #63 - BLITZCAT, #64 - ANONYMOUS, #65 - THEYSABET, #66 - QUIQUE LEE, #68 - KATE, #69 - ANONYMOUS, #70 - CRYOKINETICWOLFIES, #71 - LISA LEMONSHOOS, #72 - ANONYMOUS, #73 - ANDREA, #74 - ANDTHENWEMETTHELOCALS, #76 - MIMIAHIME, #78 - ANONYMOUS, #77 - WHALEGOD, #80 - ANONYMOUS, #81 - THETAO OF DAVID, #82 - ANONYMOUS, #83 - ANONYMOUS, #84 - NEVERFIGUREDITOUT, #85 - ARCHEMETIS, #86 - SLIGHTLYHAZARDOUS, #87 - THE-MOOGLE-OF-YOUR-NIGHTMARES, #88 - NICOLASANDTHEDIAMONDS, #89 - ANONYMOUS, #90 - GORUNNINGWITHSCISSORS, #91 - MARK, #92 - SHAKESPEAREPLAYSANDAUTUMNDAYS, #93 - SUPERDUDE100000, #94 - MELISSA, #95 - ANONYMOUS, #96 - SAM, #97 - SUNHASRISEN, #98 - CYDNEY, #99 - BABY-DEKU, #100 - CHESTER, #101 - LU

# THANK YOU ALL!

ALL RIGHTS RESERVED.
PUBLISHED IN THE UNITED STATES BY TEN SPEED PRESS,
AN IMPRINT OF CROWN PUBLISHING GROUP,
A DIVISION OF PENGUIN RANDOM HOUSE LLC, NEW YORK.
www.CROWNPUBLISHING.com
www.TENSPEED.com

TEN SPEED AND THE TEN SPEED PRESS COLOPHON ARE
REGISTERED TRADEMARKS OF PENGUIN RANDOM HOUSE LLC.

SOME COMICS APPEARED IN SLIGHTLY DIFFERENT
FORMS ON DEEPDARKFEARS.COM.

LIBRARY OF CONGRESS CATALOGING-IN-PUBLICATION
DATA IS ON FILE WITH THE PUBLISHER.

HARDCOVER ISBN: 978-1-60774-815-1
EBOOK ISBN: 978-1-60774-816-8

PRINTED IN CHINA

DESIGN BY BETSY STROMBERG

10 9 8 7 6 5 4 3 2 1

FIRST EDITION